Roundabouts

Maps and journeys

Kate Petty

and Jakki Wood

A & C Black • London

First published 1993
A & C Black (Publishers) Limited
35 Bedford Row
London WC1R 4JH

ISBN 0-7136-3708-0

© Aladdin Books Limited 1993
An Aladdin Book
designed and produced by
Aladdin Books Limited
28 Percy Street
London
WIP 9FF

A CIP catalogue record for this book
is available from the British Library

Printed in Belgium

Design David West
Children's Book Design
Illustration Jakki Wood
Text Kate Petty
Consultants Keith Lye B.A., F.R.S.G.,
Eva Bass Cert. Ed., teacher of
geography to 5-8 year-olds

Contents

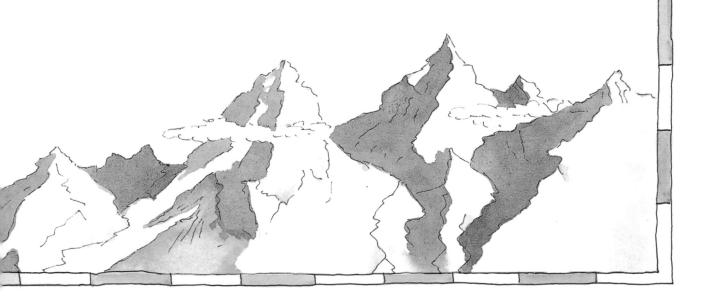

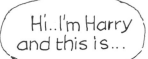

Don't get lost

Meet Harry and his dog, Ralph.
They like to travel all over the place.
Harry wants to find his way around without getting lost, so he's going to learn about maps.

Ralph, where are you?

6

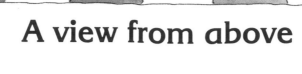

A view from above

When Harry and Ralph walk
along the street, they can't see
what's around the corner. But when they
look down from above, they can see everything laid out.
They can see the church and
the station and the house
where they live.

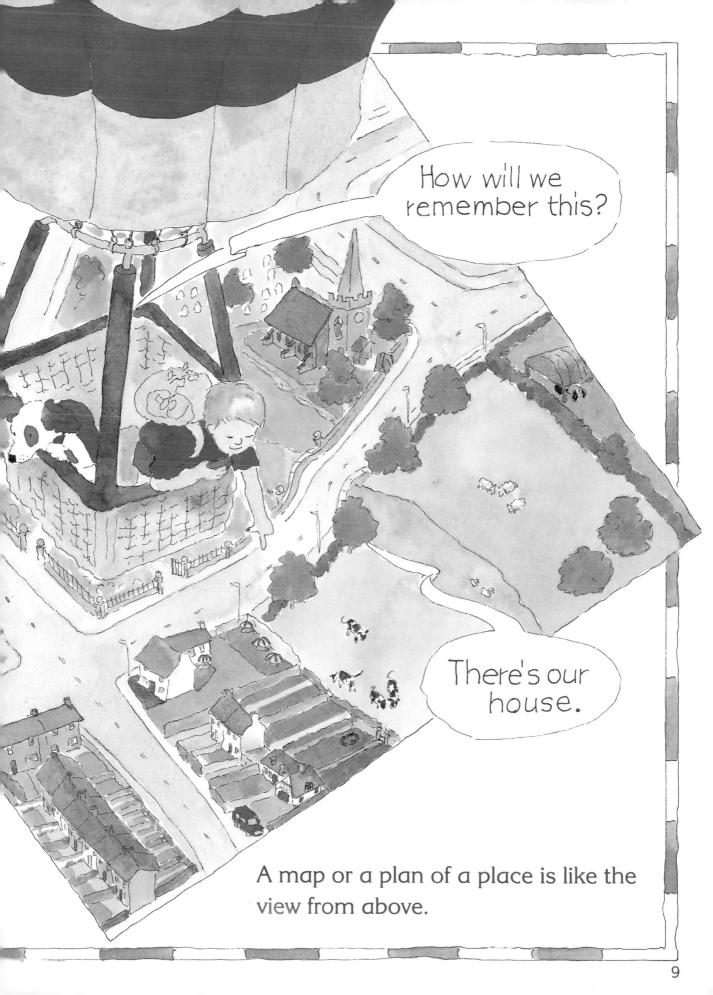

A map or a plan of a place is like the view from above.

Drawing a plan

Harry and Ralph decide to make a plan of the garden. From the balloon they can see its shape.

Harry walks from the top of the garden to the bottom. It is 30 steps long. Then he walks from one side to the other. It is 16 steps wide.

Harry draws his steps on the paper. Now he wants to put in the rose tree and the pond. How can he find out exactly where to put them?

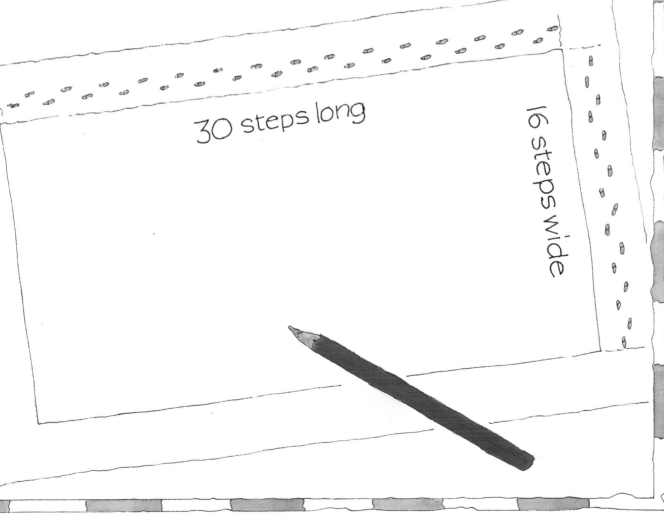

30 steps long

16 steps wide

Adding details

Harry counts his steps from one end of the garden to the rose tree - 3 steps. Then he counts his steps from the side of the garden to the rose tree - 4 steps. Ralph marks the steps on the plan and draws in the rose tree.

Then Harry finds out that the pond is 3 steps from the end and 1 step from the side. Ralph draws it in.

Ralph measures the garden with a tape measure. It is 15 metres long, which means that one of Harry's paces is half a metre (0.5 metres). They show this at the bottom of the plan. Make a plan of your garden or your classroom.

= half a metre

The journey to school

Look at the picture opposite. It shows Harry's school at the top, the church in the middle and Harry's house at the bottom. Below, Harry is making a map of his journey to school. He thinks hard about where he turns left and where he turns right. He draws in landmarks, which are special things, such as the church and the river that he sees on the way. He marks in his journey.

Don't forget the big oak tree.

Make a map of a short journey that you know well.

Street plans

Here is a street plan of the roads that Harry drew. What are the differences between the two maps? Harry's map shows landmarks which are important only to him and Ralph. The street plan has different landmarks. What are they?

It looks quite different from ours..

school

church

farm

river

footpath

park

playground

Compare your map with a street plan of the same area. What differences can you see?

Landmarks

There are different ways of showing a special feature on a map.

You can label it.  church

You can draw it.

Or you can draw a symbol, which is a special sign.

Here are some other symbols that are used on maps.

windmill

motorway

zoo

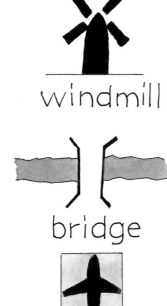
bridge

picnic

campsite

airport

wildlife park

beach

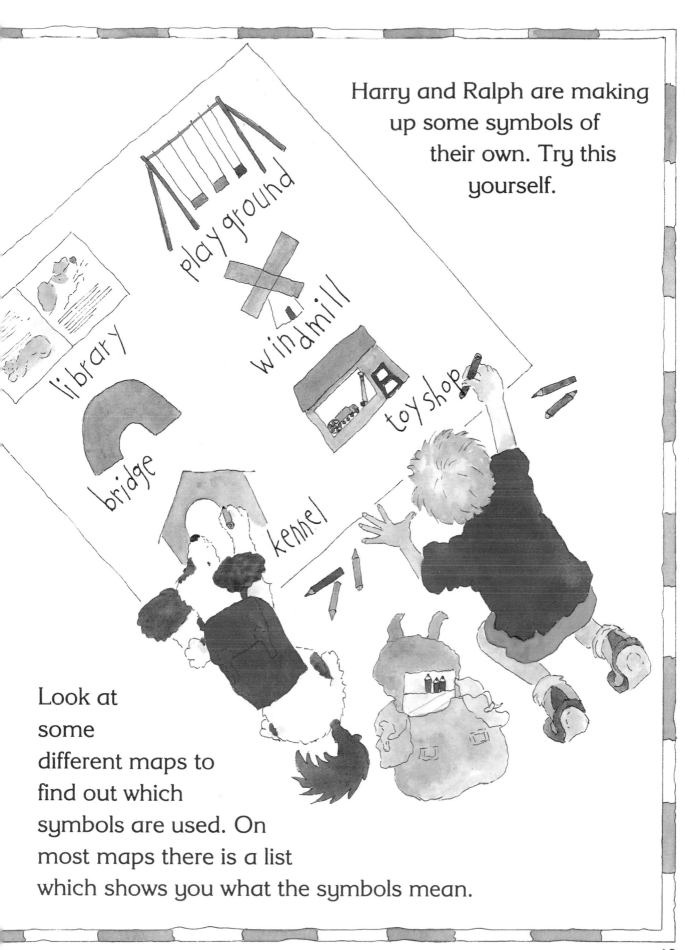

Harry and Ralph are making up some symbols of their own. Try this yourself.

playground

library

windmill

bridge

toyshop

kennel

Look at some different maps to find out which symbols are used. On most maps there is a list which shows you what the symbols mean.

North, south, east, west

Harry and Ralph understand the directions left, right, up and down. Now they want to learn about north, south, east and west. They look at a globe. The North Pole is at the top and the South Pole is at the bottom. Maps are usually drawn with north at the top, so south is at the bottom, west is left and east is right.

A magnetic compass shows you where north is.

Which direction are you facing?

12 paces west
×
12 paces south
×
15 paces south-east

Here is a map of Treasure Island. It shows how the pirates found the treasure. The direction between south and east is called south-east.

Making maps

Most modern maps are based on photographs taken from the air. A plane flies up and down the area to be mapped, just as a lawn mower is pushed up and down a lawn. A camera in the floor of the plane takes photographs of the ground beneath.

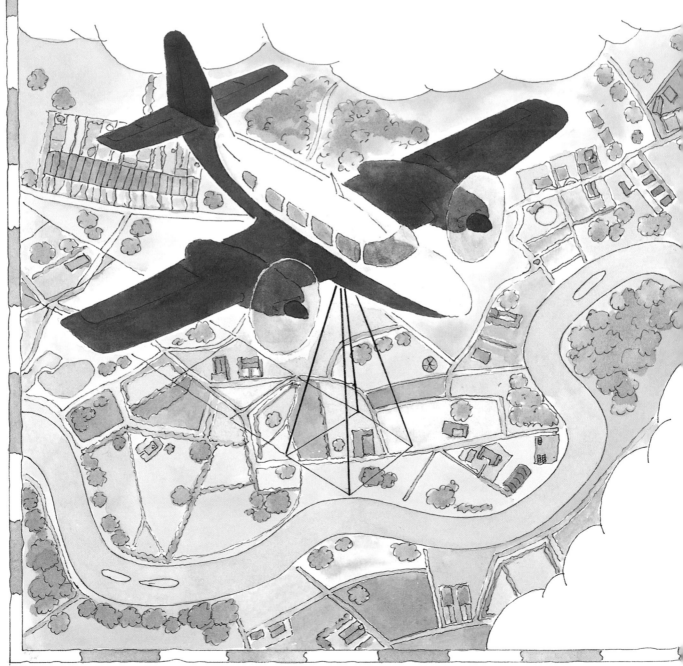

Using a map is simpler than making one.

When the photos are put together, like paving stones, the map-maker has all the information needed to start drawing a map.

That way is north.

Natural features

Every place has some feature that makes it special, and different from other places. There may be a river, or a forest, lakes or mountains. The place may be by the sea or in the middle of a huge area of land. Harry's town has a wide river running through the middle of it.

Make a list of the natural features of the place where you live. How would you show them on a map?

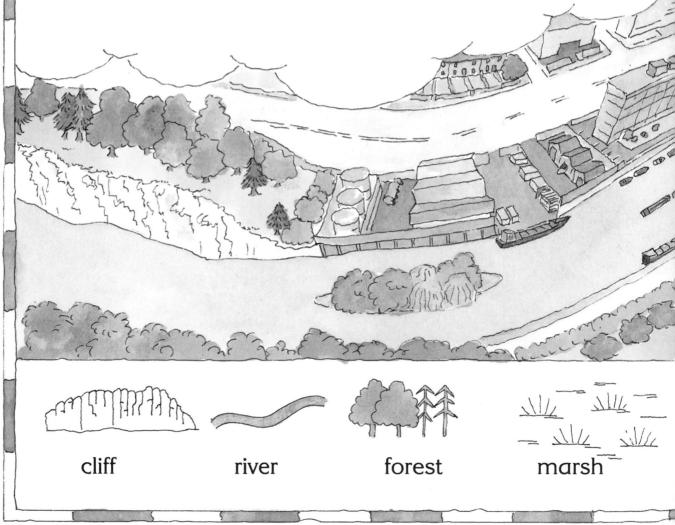

| cliff | river | forest | marsh |

Up and away

Harry and Ralph go up in their balloon to find out about the places beyond their town. They can see the town and the river. To the west the river leads to a big city and the sea. To the east there are small villages. To the north of the river there are hills. To the south there is a motorway that leads to another city, passing more towns on the way. Harry and Ralph find the landmarks on their maps.

Up and away, we're off to see the rest of the world now.

As Harry and Ralph rise higher and higher they can see
more of the ground beneath them. They need maps that
show a bigger area, drawn to a smaller scale.

Looking at an atlas

A book of maps is called an atlas. Can you find a map showing your country in an atlas? What continent is it in?
Harry and Ralph need never get lost again.

Index

This index will help you to find some of the important words in the book.